A Guide to Leading (and Surviving) the Complexities of Filipino Employees

By Angelo R. Villamejor

Table of Contents

Introduction

Chapter 1: Understanding Filipino Culture and Work Ethic (Page 7)
- Introduction to Filipino Culture
- Common Traits in the Workplace
- Cultural Nuances in Communication

Chapter 2: Navigating Common Workplace Behaviors (Page 15)
- Filipino Time
- Ningas Kugon
- Crab Mentality
- Bahala Na Habit

Chapter 3: Effective Management Strategies (Page 21)
- Building Strong Relationships
- Cultural Sensitivity and Adaptability
- Motivation and Recognition

Chapter 4: Case Studies and Practical Applications (Page 32)
- Real-Life Scenarios
- Tools and Resources
- Conclusion and Final Thoughts

Epilogue (Page 75)

Annex Section (Page 79)
- The History of the Philippines
- The Regions and the Philippines
- The Overseas Filipino Workers (OFW)
- The Global Footprint of Filipino Migrant

INTRODUCTION

The Archipelago of Diversity

Nestled in the heart of Southeast Asia, the Philippines is an archipelago of over 7,000 islands, each with its own unique charm and character. This vibrant tapestry of islands is a fitting metaphor for the diverse and dynamic nature of the Filipino workforce. Just

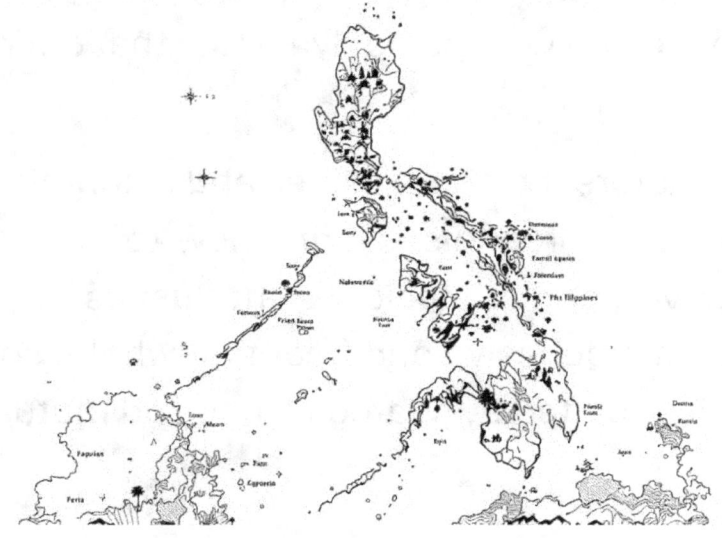

A. The Map of the Philippines with 7,000 plus Islands

as each island contributes to the rich cultural mosaic of the nation, each Filipino employee brings distinct qualities and perspectives to the workplace.

The Philippines is renowned for its breathtaking landscapes, from the emerald rice terraces of Banaue to the pristine beaches of Palawan. Similarly, the Filipino workforce is celebrated for its resilience, adaptability, and warmth. Navigating this archipelago of talents and traits can be as thrilling and rewarding as exploring the islands themselves.

In "A Guide to Leading (and Surviving) the Complexities of Filipino Employees," we embark on a journey through this diverse landscape. Much like navigating the intricate waterways and terrains of the islands, leading Filipino employees requires understanding, adaptability, and a touch of adventure. Each chapter of this book serves as a compass, guiding you through the cultural nuances and workplace dynamics that define the Filipino experience.

Join us as we explore the complexities and celebrate the strengths of the Filipino workforce, discovering how to lead with empathy, cultural sensitivity, and strategic insight. Just as the islands of the Philippines form a cohesive and beautiful whole, so too can your team thrive when united by shared values and mutual respect.

Embracing the Complexities of the Filipino Workforce

In the vibrant and diverse landscape of global business, the Filipino workforce stands out for its unique blend of warmth, resilience, and adaptability. As the world becomes increasingly interconnected, understanding the cultural nuances and complexities of different employee groups is essential for effective leadership and management. This book, "A Guide to Leading (and Surviving) the Complexities of Filipino Employees," aims to provide valuable insights into managing Filipino workers, drawing from both cultural understanding and practical experience.

Managing a group of Filipino employees can sometimes feel like navigating a labyrinth. While Filipino employees are often loving and nurturing, bringing a sense of family and community into the workplace, they can also introduce certain cultural habits that may pose challenges to managers. Behaviors such as "Filipino Time," "Ningas Kugon," "Crab Mentality," and the "Bahala Na" attitude can impact productivity and team dynamics if not effectively managed.

This book is not only a resource for local managers but also for foreign managers who lead Filipino workers scattered across the globe. With an estimated 2.2 million Overseas Filipino Workers (OFWs) contributing to various industries worldwide, understanding their cultural background becomes crucial for fostering effective and harmonious working relationships.

Through real-world examples and practical guidance, we aim to equip you with the tools needed to lead with empathy, cultural sensitivity, and strategic foresight. By understanding and embracing the unique qualities of the Filipino workforce, you can unlock new levels of collaboration, creativity, and achievement within your organization.

As you embark on this journey of discovery, remember that cultural diversity is not a barrier but a bridge to innovation and success. Join us as we delve into the rich tapestry of Filipino culture and uncover the secrets to successfully leading Filipino employees. Whether you are a seasoned manager or new to the role, this guide will serve as a valuable resource in your leadership journey.

Chapter 1:

Understanding Filipino Culture and Work Ethic

Introduction to Filipino Culture

Welcome to the Philippines, where the people are as warm as the tropical sun and as resilient as the bamboo trees swaying in the breeze. Managing Filipino employees is like embarking on an exciting adventure filled with laughter, camaraderie, and yes, a few quirky challenges that make the journey all the more interesting.

Imagine this: you're a manager, and your team is a lively bunch who greet you with smiles that could light up the darkest of days. They're known for their hospitality, and you quickly learn that "mi casa es su casa" is practically a national motto. *("Mi casa es su casa" is a Spanish phrase that translates to "My house is your house" in English. It's often used to express hospitality and a welcoming attitude, indicating that guests should feel at home and comfortable. While it's a Spanish expression, it captures the essence of Filipino hospitality, where making others feel welcome and part of the family is highly valued).* But as you sip your morning coffee, you also realize that navigating this vibrant culture requires a special kind of map—one that we're about to unfold together.

In the Philippines, family isn't just important—it's everything. It's the North Star guiding every decision, big or small. This deep-rooted sense of family extends beyond bloodlines, encompassing friends, colleagues, and even the friendly neighborhood stray dog. For managers, this means understanding that when you hire one Filipino employee, you get an entire village cheering them on.

This strong sense of community translates into the workplace as a profound sense of teamwork and support. It's like having a team of Avengers, each with their unique superpower, ready to assist and uplift one another. As a manager, tapping into this collective energy can lead to extraordinary results.

Common Traits in the Workplace: The Good, the Quirky, and the Adorable

Filipino employees are renowned for their adaptability, resilience, and a smile that can melt the iciest of hearts. But let's dive a little deeper into these traits and discover the delightful quirks that come with them.

- **Hospitality with a Capital H**: Imagine walking into the office and being greeted with a chorus of "Good morning, po!" and offers of snacks that range from local delicacies to the occasional mystery dish. It's like having a daily potluck where everyone is invited. Just be prepared for the inevitable food coma!

- **Adaptability Extraordinaire**: Filipinos possess the magical ability to adapt to any situation, much like chameleons but with a lot more flair. Whether it's a sudden change in project direction or an impromptu karaoke session at lunch, they're ready to roll with the punches and hit the high notes.

- **Resilience, Thy Name is Filipino**: If resilience were an Olympic sport, Filipinos would bring home the gold every time. From typhoons to traffic jams, nothing seems to dampen their spirits. They're like the Energizer bunnies of the workforce, always bouncing back with optimism and a hearty laugh.

Cultural Nuances in Communication: The Art of Indirectness

Communication in the Filipino context is an art form, a delicate dance of words and gestures that requires a keen eye and a gentle touch. Here, "hiya" (shame) plays a starring role, and saving face is a top priority.

- **The Subtle Symphony of Indirectness**: Filipinos have mastered the art of saying "no" without actually uttering the word. It's like a game of charades where everyone knows the rules. As a manager, learning to read between the lines is key to understanding your team's true sentiments.

- **Building Trust: The Secret Ingredient**: Trust is the secret sauce that binds Filipino relationships. It's earned through respect, fairness, and a genuine interest in your team's well-being. Once established, it opens the door to honest conversations and a harmonious work environment.

The Filipino Time Phenomenon: A Love-Hate Relationship

Ah, Filipino Time—a concept that can either be the bane of a manager's existence or a charming quirk, depending on how you look at it. Filipino Time is a cultural phenomenon where time is more of a suggestion than a strict rule. It's the reason why "I'll be there in five minutes" could mean anything from fifteen minutes to an hour.

But before you pull your hair out in frustration, let's explore the roots of this behavior. Filipino Time is deeply intertwined with the cultural values of flexibility and relational harmony. In a culture where maintaining relationships is paramount, being late is often overlooked in favor of ensuring that everyone feels valued and included.

For managers, understanding this cultural nuance is crucial. While punctuality is important, it's equally vital to approach the situation with empathy and humor. Consider setting clear expectations and gently reminding your team of the importance of timeliness. And if all else fails, embrace the unpredictability with a smile and a Plan B.

Ningas Kugon: The Flickering Flame

"Ningas Kugon" is a term that describes the initial enthusiasm that fizzles out over time—much like a grass fire that starts strong but quickly dies down. It's a behavior that can be challenging for managers, especially when trying to sustain momentum on long-term projects.

The key to managing Ningas Kugon lies in understanding its roots. Filipinos are passionate and energetic, often diving headfirst into new ventures with gusto. However, sustaining that energy requires consistent motivation and engagement.

As a manager, consider implementing strategies that keep the flame burning. Break down projects into smaller, manageable tasks with regular check-ins and celebrations of progress. Encourage open communication and provide opportunities for team members to share their ideas and feedback. By nurturing a culture of continuous engagement, you can turn Ningas Kugon into a steady, enduring flame.

Crab Mentality: Turning Competition into Collaboration

Crab Mentality is a term that describes the desire to pull others down when they succeed, much like crabs in a bucket. It's a behavior that can hinder teamwork and collaboration, but with the right approach, it can be transformed into a positive force.

Understanding the roots of Crab Mentality is essential. In a culture where community and belonging are highly valued, competition can sometimes be perceived as a threat to unity. However, by fostering a culture of collaboration and mutual support, managers can turn this mentality into a strength.

Encourage transparency and open communication within your team. Celebrate individual and collective achievements and emphasize the value of working together towards common goals. By creating an environment where everyone feels valued and supported, you can transform competition into a powerful tool for growth and success.

Bahala Na: Embracing Uncertainty with Confidence

"Bahala Na" is a phrase that embodies a sense of fatalism—leaving things to fate and trusting that everything will work out in the end. While it can be a source of frustration for managers, it's also a testament to the Filipino spirit of resilience and adaptability.

The Bahala Na attitude is rooted in the cultural value of flexibility and acceptance of uncertainty. In a world where change is constant, Filipinos have learned to embrace the unknown with confidence and optimism.

As a manager, harnessing the positive aspects of Bahala Na can lead to a more resilient and adaptable team. Encourage your employees to take calculated risks and explore new possibilities. Provide support and guidance while allowing room for creativity and innovation. By embracing uncertainty with confidence, you can unlock new levels of potential and growth within your team.

Conclusion: Celebrating the Filipino Workforce

As we conclude this chapter, it's important to celebrate the unique qualities that make the Filipino workforce a valuable asset to any organization. From their warmth and hospitality to their resilience and adaptability, Filipino employees bring a wealth of strengths to the table.

For managers, both foreign and local, understanding and embracing these cultural nuances is key to unlocking the full potential of their teams. By approaching the complexities of managing Filipino employees with empathy, humor, and cultural sensitivity, you can create a work environment that fosters collaboration, innovation, and success.

So, whether you're managing a team in the bustling streets of Manila or leading a group of OFWs across the globe, remember that the journey is as rewarding as the destination. Embrace the adventure, celebrate the quirks, and enjoy the ride. After all, in the world of work, it's the people who make the journey truly unforgettable.

Chapter 2:
Navigating Common Workplace Behaviors

Introduction: Embracing the Quirks

Welcome back to the vibrant world of the Filipino workplace, where every day is a new adventure filled with unique behaviors and delightful quirks. As a manager, understanding these common workplace behaviors is like learning the secret handshake to a club—once you master it, you're in for a rewarding and harmonious working relationship.

In this chapter, we'll dive into the intricacies of behaviors like Filipino Time, Ningas Kugon, Crab Mentality, and the Bahala Na attitude. We'll explore how these cultural traits can impact the workplace and, more importantly, how you can navigate them with grace, humor, and a touch of creativity.

Filipino Time: A Cultural Phenomenon

Ah, Filipino Time—a concept that has baffled many a punctual soul. Imagine scheduling a meeting for 9 AM and realizing that the clock strikes 9:15 AM before everyone strolls in with a cheerful "Good morning!" Filipino Time is more than just a habit; it's a cultural phenomenon deeply rooted in the values of flexibility and relational harmony.

While this relaxed approach to time can be a source of frustration, it also offers an opportunity to embrace flexibility and adaptability. As a manager, setting clear expectations and gently reminding your team of the importance of punctuality can help bridge the gap between cultural norms and workplace efficiency. And remember, a little humor goes a long way—consider setting meeting times 15 minutes earlier than planned, and watch the magic unfold.

Ningas Kugon: Sustaining the Flame

"Ningas Kugon" is a term that describes the initial burst of enthusiasm that fizzles out over time. It's like starting a marathon with a sprint, only to realize halfway through that you're out of breath. This behavior can be challenging for managers, especially when trying to maintain momentum on long-term projects.

The key to managing Ningas Kugon lies in understanding its roots. Filipinos are passionate and energetic, often diving headfirst into new ventures with gusto. However, sustaining that energy requires consistent motivation and engagement.

Consider implementing strategies that keep the flame burning. Break down projects into smaller, manageable tasks with regular check-ins and celebrations of progress. Encourage open communication and provide opportunities for team members to share their ideas and feedback. By nurturing a culture of continuous engagement, you can turn Ningas Kugon into a steady, enduring flame.

Crab Mentality: Fostering Collaboration

Crab Mentality, a term that describes the desire to pull others down when they succeed, is a behavior that can hinder teamwork and collaboration. But fear not—this mentality can be transformed into a positive force with the right approach.

Understanding the roots of Crab Mentality is essential. In a culture where community and belonging are highly valued, competition can sometimes be perceived as a threat to unity. However, by fostering a culture of collaboration and mutual support, managers can turn this mentality into a strength.

Encourage transparency and open communication within your team. Celebrate individual and collective achievements and emphasize the value of working together towards common goals. By creating an environment where everyone feels valued and supported, you can transform competition into a powerful tool for growth and success.

Bahala Na: Embracing Uncertainty

"Bahala Na" is a phrase that embodies a sense of fatalism—leaving things to fate and trusting that everything will work out in the end. While it can be a source of frustration for managers, it's also a testament to the Filipino spirit of resilience and adaptability.

The Bahala Na attitude is rooted in the cultural value of flexibility and acceptance of uncertainty. In a world where change is constant, Filipinos have learned to embrace the unknown with confidence and optimism.

As a manager, harnessing the positive aspects of Bahala Na can lead to a more resilient and adaptable team. Encourage your employees to take calculated risks and explore new possibilities. Provide support and guidance while allowing room for creativity and innovation. By embracing uncertainty with confidence, you can unlock new levels of potential and growth within your team.

Conclusion: Celebrating Diversity

As we wrap up this exploration of common workplace behaviors, it's essential to recognize the diversity and richness that Filipino culture brings to the workplace. Each behavior, from Filipino Time to Bahala Na, presents unique challenges and opportunities for growth and understanding.

For managers, whether you're navigating the vibrant streets of Manila or coordinating with teams across the globe, embracing these cultural nuances is crucial. By fostering an environment of empathy, humor, and open-mindedness, you can transform these challenges into strengths, creating a dynamic and cohesive team.

Remember, the journey of leadership is filled with learning and adaptation. Celebrate the quirks and differences that make your team unique and use them as a foundation for building a supportive and innovative workplace. In the end, it's the diverse perspectives and experiences of your team members that will drive success and make your leadership journey truly rewarding.

Chapter 3:
Effective Management Strategies for Filipino Employees

Introduction: Crafting the Perfect Recipe for Success

Welcome to the next chapter of your leadership journey, where we dive into the art of crafting effective management strategies for Filipino employees. Think of this as a culinary adventure, where each strategy is an ingredient in a recipe for success. With the right blend of empathy, cultural understanding, and innovative thinking, you'll create a harmonious and productive work environment that brings out the best in your Filipino team.

In this chapter, we'll explore strategies that not only address the unique challenges of managing Filipino employees but also leverage their strengths to drive success. From building strong relationships to fostering motivation and recognition, we'll equip you with the tools needed to navigate the complexities of leadership with confidence and flair.

Building Strong Relationships: The Heart of Leadership

In the Philippines, relationships are the heart and soul of both personal and professional life. As a manager, building strong relationships with your team is akin to planting a garden—nurture it with care, and it will flourish.

The Power of Connection: Establishing a genuine connection with your Filipino employees is the foundation of a strong relationship. Take the time to understand their aspirations, challenges, and interests. Whether it's sharing a meal or engaging in casual conversations, these moments of connection lay the groundwork for trust and mutual respect. And remember, a little humor goes a long way—nothing breaks the ice like a good joke about the latest teleserye (soap opera) plot twist!

The Role of Empathy: Empathy is the secret ingredient that elevates a manager from good to great. In the context of Filipino employees, where emotions play a significant role in daily interactions, empathy becomes even more crucial. By stepping into your employees' shoes, you gain valuable insights into their perspectives and motivations, allowing you to offer support and guidance that truly resonates with their needs.

Demonstrating empathy not only touches the hearts of your Filipino team members but also paves the way to earning their trust. This trust is fundamental to building strong, collaborative relationships. In Filipino culture, the concept of "utang-na-loob" reflects a deep sense of gratitude and obligation to reciprocate kindness. When you show genuine empathy, expect it to be reciprocated, as Filipinos naturally feel compelled to return the favor.

By fostering an empathetic environment, you create a workplace where mutual respect and understanding thrive, ultimately leading to a more cohesive and motivated team. Remember, empathy isn't just about understanding—it's about building connections that inspire loyalty and commitment.

Celebrating Milestones: In a culture that values community and togetherness, celebrating milestones is a cherished tradition. Whether it's a work anniversary, a project completion, or a personal achievement, take the time to acknowledge and celebrate these moments. A simple gesture of appreciation goes a long way in strengthening relationships and boosting morale. And don't forget the pancit (noodles)—it's a must-have for any celebration! And lastly, since Filipinos love celebrations, this can sometimes lead to a karaoke session to belt out a classic OPM (Original Pilipino Music) hit—just be prepared for some friendly teasing about your singing skills!

Cultural Sensitivity and Adaptability: Embracing Diversity

Cultural sensitivity and adaptability are the spices that add flavor to your management style. In a diverse workplace, embracing cultural nuances is essential for fostering an inclusive and harmonious environment.

Understanding Cultural Contexts: The Philippines is a vibrant tapestry of over 7,000 islands, divided into 18 regions, each with its own distinct language and cultural heritage. This diversity means that every Filipino employee brings a unique cultural background to the workplace. As a leader, taking the time to learn about and appreciate

these differences is invaluable. Understanding the significance of family and community in Filipino culture is crucial. These elements are deeply ingrained and influence how employees interact and collaborate. By recognizing these cultural nuances, you enhance your ability to lead effectively and foster a supportive work environment.

If you ever find yourself puzzled by a cultural reference or tradition, don't hesitate to ask. Filipinos are often eager to share stories about their rich traditions and customs. This openness not only enriches your understanding but also strengthens the bond between you and your team, creating a more cohesive and harmonious workplace. Embrace this diversity as a strength, and let it guide you in building a dynamic and inclusive team.

Adapting Your Management Style. Flexibility is a cornerstone of successful leadership, especially when managing a diverse team. To effectively lead your Filipino employees, it's crucial to adapt your management style to align with their cultural context and individual needs. This adaptability not only demonstrates respect and consideration but also fosters a sense of belonging and acceptance within the team.

While flexibility allows Filipino employees to perform in ways that suit them best, it's important to maintain high expectations to ensure consistent performance. Filipinos are naturally loving and friendly, which can sometimes blur the lines between professional and personal relationships. As their leader, it's essential to find the right balance between being approachable and maintaining the standards necessary for achieving organizational goals.

To achieve this balance, establish clear expectations and communicate them in a way that resonates with your team. Encourage open communication and provide constructive feedback that reinforces both flexibility and accountability. By doing so, you can create an environment where Filipino employees feel valued and motivated, while also striving for excellence in their work. Remember, effective leadership is about nurturing both the personal and professional growth of your team members.

Encouraging Open Dialogue: Creating an environment where open dialogue is encouraged and valued is essential for fostering a culture of transparency and communication. By empowering your Filipino employees to voice their ideas, concerns, and feedback, you not only strengthen relationships but also drive innovation and collaboration.

However, it's important to recognize that Filipinos tend to be more "personal" rather than strictly "professional" in their interactions. This means that the way you communicate with them is crucial. A direct or confrontational approach may not be effective. Instead, consider rephrasing your sentences and being mindful of your word choices to ensure they are received positively.

Understanding the historical context of the Philippines can provide valuable insights into this communication style. The country has a history of colonization and struggles for independence, such as the revolution sparked by Jose Rizal's influential novel and the People Power Revolution of 1986. These events highlight the power of emotional resonance and the importance of touching hearts to inspire action.

When communicating with Filipino employees, aim to connect with them on a personal level. Show empathy, respect, and genuine interest in their well-being. By doing so, you can foster a sense of loyalty and support that encourages them to follow and collaborate with you wholeheartedly. Remember, effective communication is not just about conveying information—it's about building trust and understanding.

Motivation and Recognition: Fueling the Fire

Motivation and recognition are the fuel that keeps the engine of your team running smoothly. By understanding what drives your employees and acknowledging their contributions, you create a positive and dynamic work environment.

Understanding Motivational Drivers: Each employee is motivated by different factors, whether it's personal growth, financial incentives, or a sense of purpose. For many Filipino employees, family plays a significant role as a motivational driver. The desire to provide for loved ones and achieve a better quality of life often fuels their dedication and hard work. Take the time to identify these drivers and tailor your approach accordingly. For instance, offering flexible work arrangements or family-oriented benefits can resonate well with Filipino employees, enhancing their engagement and motivation. This personalized approach ensures that your team remains committed and inspired.

And if all else fails, remember that a well-timed joke or a round of merienda (snack time) can do wonders for morale! Sharing a laugh and some delicious snacks can create a sense of camaraderie and uplift spirits, reinforcing the bonds within your team.

The Art of Recognition: Recognition is a powerful tool for boosting morale and fostering a sense of accomplishment, particularly among Filipino employees who thrive on affirmation and appreciation. A study by Gallup found that employees who receive regular recognition are more productive, engaged, and likely to stay with their organization. This is especially true in the Filipino context, where acknowledgment of hard work is deeply valued.

Whether it's a public acknowledgment during a team meeting or a private note of appreciation, recognizing your employees' efforts reinforces their value and contribution to the organization. For instance, celebrating a team member's innovative solution to a problem or their dedication to a project can significantly uplift their spirits and motivate others.

And remember, adding a touch of humor to your recognition can make it even more memorable. Consider playful awards like "The Most Creative Problem Solver" or "The Best Team Spirit Cheerleader." These lighthearted acknowledgments not only boost morale but also create a positive and enjoyable work atmosphere. Recognition, when done thoughtfully, can transform your workplace into a thriving and motivated community.

Creating a Culture of Appreciation: Cultivating a culture where appreciation is a core value can have a profound impact on your team. Encouraging team members to recognize and celebrate each other's achievements fosters a supportive and uplifting environment. Research by the Harvard Business Review highlights that appreciation significantly enhances job satisfaction and strengthens team cohesion and collaboration. When employees feel valued, they are more likely to engage positively with their work and colleagues.

In the Filipino context, appreciation often goes hand-in-hand with communal celebrations. Whether it's a simple merienda or a grand fiesta, Filipinos know how to celebrate achievements with joy and camaraderie. These gatherings not only honor individual and team successes but also reinforce the bonds within the group.

By embedding appreciation into your organizational culture, you create a workplace where employees feel acknowledged and motivated. This, in turn, leads to higher levels of engagement, productivity, and overall satisfaction. So, don't hesitate to celebrate successes—big or small—with a feast or a heartfelt acknowledgment. It's these moments of appreciation that build a thriving and cohesive team.

Empowering Your Team: The Path to Success

Empowerment is the key to unlocking your team's full potential. By providing your employees with the tools, resources, and autonomy they need, you foster a sense of ownership and accountability. Research from the Harvard Business Review indicates that empowered teams are more engaged and productive, leading to better organizational outcomes.

Delegating with Confidence. Delegation is an essential skill for effective leadership. Trusting your employees to take on responsibilities and make decisions empowers them to own their work and contribute significantly to the organization's success. A study by Gallup found that managers who delegate effectively can increase their team's performance by up to 33%. This is particularly relevant for Filipino employees, who often thrive in environments that value trust and autonomy.

In the Filipino workplace, delegation can be particularly effective when aligned with cultural values such as "bayanihan," the spirit of communal unity and cooperation. For example, assigning team members to lead specific aspects of a project not only empowers them but also fosters a sense of shared responsibility and collaboration. This approach resonates with Filipino employees, who often excel when they feel their contributions are part of a collective effort.

Moreover, incorporating humor into delegation can enhance engagement and creativity. Consider setting up a friendly competition to see who can devise the most innovative solution to a project challenge. Filipinos, known for their love of fun and camaraderie, will likely appreciate this approach, leading to a more dynamic and motivated team.

By delegating with confidence and cultural awareness, you create an empowering environment that leverages the strengths of your Filipino employees, driving both individual and organizational success.

Encouraging Innovation and Creativity. Creating an environment where innovation and creativity are encouraged and celebrated is crucial for fostering a dynamic and forward-thinking team. According to a report by McKinsey, organizations that prioritize innovation are more likely to achieve long-term growth. This is especially relevant for Filipino employees, who often bring a rich blend of creativity and resourcefulness to the workplace.

To encourage innovation among Filipino employees, consider integrating cultural practices that resonate with their strengths. For example, the Filipino concept of "diskarte," which refers to resourcefulness and adaptability, can be harnessed by providing opportunities for team members to brainstorm solutions to real-world challenges. This not only taps into their innate creativity but also empowers them to contribute meaningfully to the organization.

Additionally, fostering a collaborative environment that values diverse perspectives can lead to innovative breakthroughs.

Encourage cross-departmental projects or "idea hackathons" where employees can work together to explore new concepts. Filipinos, known for their strong sense of community and teamwork, will likely thrive in such settings, resulting in creative solutions that benefit the entire organization.

Supporting Professional Development. Investing in your employees' professional growth and development is a powerful way to demonstrate your commitment to their success. A study by LinkedIn Learning found that 94% of employees would stay longer at a company that invests in their career development. This is particularly significant for Filipino employees, who often value opportunities for learning and advancement as part of their career journey.

To effectively support professional development among Filipino employees, consider offering tailored training programs that align with their career goals. For example, providing workshops on skills that are in high demand, such as digital marketing or project management, can enhance their expertise and confidence. Additionally, mentorship programs that pair experienced employees with newer team members can foster knowledge sharing and personal growth, resonating with the Filipino value of "pakikisama" or camaraderie.

Career advancement opportunities are also highly valued. Encourage Filipino employees to take on leadership roles in projects or initiatives, allowing them to showcase their abilities and prepare for future promotions. This not only boosts their morale but also reinforces their loyalty to the organization.

And don't forget to sprinkle in some humor during training sessions—laughter is a great way to break the ice and make learning enjoyable. Filipinos, known for their cheerful disposition, will appreciate a light-hearted approach that makes professional development both engaging and fun. By investing in their growth, you cultivate a motivated and committed workforce that contributes to the long-term success of your organization.

Conclusion: The Journey of Leadership

As we conclude this chapter, it's important to recognize that effective management is an ongoing journey of learning, growth, and adaptation. By embracing the unique qualities and strengths of your Filipino team, you create a work environment that fosters collaboration, innovation, and success.

Remember, leadership is not just about achieving goals; it's about inspiring and empowering others to reach their full potential. By crafting a management style that blends empathy, cultural sensitivity, and strategic thinking, you pave the way for a rewarding and fulfilling leadership journey.

Chapter 4:
Case Studies and Practical Applications

Introduction: Bridging Theory and Practice

As we embark on the final chapter of this guide, we find ourselves at the intersection of theory and practice—a place where knowledge meets action and understanding transforms into tangible results. This chapter is dedicated to exploring real-life scenarios and practical applications that illuminate the complexities and nuances of managing Filipino employees in diverse work environments.

In today's globalized world, the ability to navigate cultural diversity is more important than ever. Filipino employees, with their unique blend of cultural traits and work ethics, present both opportunities and challenges for managers striving to foster inclusive and productive workplaces. By delving into these case studies, we aim to provide you with a comprehensive understanding of the dynamics at play and equip you with the tools needed to lead effectively.

Understanding the Filipino Workforce

The Filipino workforce is renowned for its adaptability, resilience, and warmth. These qualities, deeply rooted in the country's rich cultural heritage, contribute to the unique dynamics of Filipino employees. However, managing a team that embodies such diversity requires more than just an understanding of cultural traits; it demands an appreciation of the individual experiences and perspectives that each employee brings to the table.

Throughout this chapter, we will examine various scenarios that highlight the challenges faced by managers and the innovative solutions they have implemented to overcome them. From addressing the infamous "Filipino Time" to navigating the intricacies of "Ningas Kugon," these case studies offer valuable insights into the real-world applications of the concepts discussed in previous chapters.

The Importance of Cultural Sensitivity

At the heart of effective management lies cultural sensitivity—the ability to recognize, respect, and adapt to the cultural nuances that influence employee behavior and interactions. By fostering an environment of empathy and understanding, managers can bridge the gap between cultural differences and create a cohesive and harmonious workplace.

As we explore these case studies, you will see how cultural sensitivity plays a pivotal role in addressing challenges and driving success. From flexible scheduling systems to fostering a culture of accountability and recognition, the strategies employed by these managers demonstrate the power of cultural awareness in enhancing team performance and morale.

Innovative Solutions for Complex Challenges

The complexities of managing Filipino employees are not insurmountable; they present opportunities for innovation and growth. Through the lens of these case studies, we will uncover the creative solutions that have enabled managers to turn challenges into strengths. Whether it's leveraging technology to enhance communication or implementing peer recognition programs to boost morale, these examples showcase the transformative impact of strategic leadership.

A Roadmap for Success

This chapter serves as a roadmap for navigating the intricacies of managing a culturally diverse team. By learning from the experiences of others, you can gain valuable insights into the best practices and strategies that drive success. As you apply these lessons to your own leadership journey, remember that the key to effective management lies in embracing diversity as a strength and fostering an environment where every employee feels valued and empowered.

Real-Life Scenarios: Learning from Experience

In the world of management, there's no substitute for experience. Let's dive into some real-life scenarios that highlight the unique challenges and triumphs of managing Filipino teams.

Case Study 1:
Navigating Filipino Time in a Global Company

Introduction: The Challenge of Filipino Time

Maria, a project manager at a multinational corporation based in Manila, faced a common yet challenging cultural phenomenon known as "Filipino Time." Her team, renowned for their creativity and dedication, often struggled with punctuality. Meetings scheduled for 9 AM frequently began at 9:15 or later, and deadlines were sometimes perceived as flexible suggestions rather than firm commitments. This cultural trait, deeply rooted in the values of flexibility and relational harmony, posed a significant challenge in a global business environment where time is often equated with money.

Understanding Filipino Time

To effectively address this issue, Maria first sought to understand the cultural underpinnings of Filipino Time. In Filipino culture, relationships and social harmony often take precedence over strict adherence to time. This cultural nuance is not unique to the Philippines; similar attitudes towards time can be found in other cultures where personal relationships are highly valued. However, in the context of a global company, where teams from different cultural backgrounds collaborate, this relaxed approach to time management can lead to misunderstandings and inefficiencies.

The Impact on Productivity

The impact of Filipino Time on productivity was evident. Delayed meetings and extended deadlines disrupted workflows and created bottlenecks in project timelines. Maria observed that while her team excelled in creativity and problem-solving, the lack of punctuality sometimes hindered their ability to meet client expectations and project goals. Recognizing the need for change, Maria embarked on a journey to find a solution that respected cultural values while enhancing productivity.

Implementing a Flexible Scheduling System

Maria's strategy began with the implementation of a flexible scheduling system. Drawing from research on cross-cultural management, she understood that imposing strict time constraints might not be effective. Instead, she introduced buffer times for meetings and deadlines, allowing for a degree of flexibility while maintaining overall project timelines. This approach was informed by studies that highlight the importance of cultural sensitivity in international business settings (Hofstede, 2010).

Emphasizing the Importance of Punctuality

In addition to flexible scheduling, Maria emphasized the importance of punctuality in a culturally sensitive manner. She organized workshops and team-building activities to foster a shared understanding of time management. These sessions, inspired by the work of Trompenaars and Hampden-Turner (1997), focused on bridging cultural differences and highlighting the benefits of punctuality in achieving team goals.

Creating a Culture of Accountability

To further support her efforts, Maria introduced a culture of accountability. She encouraged team members to take ownership of their schedules and responsibilities. By promoting self-management and peer accountability, the team gradually developed a sense of collective responsibility for meeting deadlines. This shift in mindset was supported by research from the Harvard Business Review, which suggests that accountability can significantly enhance team performance (Harvard Business Review, 2018).

Leveraging Technology for Time Management

Maria also leveraged technology to improve time management. She introduced digital tools like Trello and Slack to facilitate communication and task tracking. These tools provided real-time updates on project progress and deadlines, helping team members stay organized and informed. The integration of technology was supported by studies that demonstrate the positive impact of digital tools on productivity and collaboration (McKinsey & Company, 2020).

Balancing Flexibility and Structure

A key aspect of Maria's approach was finding the right balance between flexibility and structure. She recognized that while flexibility was important, it needed to be balanced with clear expectations and boundaries. By setting realistic deadlines and providing the necessary resources and support, Maria ensured that her team could work efficiently without feeling overwhelmed.

The Role of Leadership in Cultural Adaptation

Maria's leadership played a crucial role in navigating Filipino Time. Her ability to adapt her management style to suit the cultural context of her team was instrumental in achieving success. By demonstrating empathy and understanding, Maria built trust and rapport with her team, fostering a positive work environment where cultural differences were respected and valued.

Outcomes and Lessons Learned

The implementation of flexible scheduling and culturally sensitive time management strategies yielded positive results. Maria's team experienced improved punctuality and productivity, leading to enhanced client satisfaction and project outcomes. The success of this approach was reflected in the team's ability to meet deadlines consistently without compromising their creativity and morale.

Maria's experience underscores the importance of cultural sensitivity and adaptability in managing diverse teams. By understanding and embracing cultural nuances, leaders can create inclusive workplaces that leverage the strengths of their employees. This case study serves as a valuable lesson for managers navigating similar challenges in multicultural settings.

Conclusion: A Model for Success

Maria's journey in navigating Filipino Time offers a model for success in managing cultural diversity in the workplace. Her approach highlights the importance of balancing flexibility with structure, fostering a culture of accountability, and leveraging technology to enhance productivity. By respecting cultural values and promoting open communication, Maria successfully transformed a challenge into an opportunity for growth and innovation.

As organizations continue to expand globally, the ability to navigate cultural complexities will become increasingly important. Maria's experience demonstrates that with the right strategies and mindset, leaders can harness the power of cultural diversity to drive success and achieve organizational goals.

Case Study 2:
Overcoming Ningas Kugon in a Start-up Environment

Introduction: The Challenge of Ningas Kugon

In the fast-paced world of tech start-ups, maintaining momentum and enthusiasm is crucial for success. Juan, a project manager at a burgeoning tech start-up, faced the challenge of Ningas Kugon—a cultural phenomenon characterized by an initial burst of enthusiasm that quickly fades. This behavior, while common in various cultural contexts, can significantly impact long-term objectives and project success if not effectively managed.

Understanding Ningas Kugon

Ningas Kugon, a term rooted in Filipino culture, refers to the tendency to start projects with great enthusiasm, only to lose interest and motivation over time. This behavior is often compared to a grass fire that burns brightly at first but quickly dies down. In the context of a start-up, where innovation and sustained effort are key, overcoming Ningas Kugon is essential to achieving long-term goals.

The Impact on Productivity and Innovation

Juan observed that while his team of developers was highly skilled and creative, their initial excitement for new projects often waned, leading to delays and unfinished tasks. This lack of sustained motivation not only affected productivity but also hindered the team's ability to innovate and deliver on ambitious objectives. Recognizing the need for a solution, Juan set out to address this challenge head-on.

Implementing Regular Brainstorming Sessions

One of Juan's first strategies was to introduce regular brainstorming sessions. Research by Amabile and Kramer (2011) highlights the importance of creative collaboration in fostering innovation and maintaining motivation. By providing a platform for team members to share ideas and explore new concepts, Juan encouraged continuous engagement and a sense of ownership over projects.

These sessions were designed to be open and inclusive, allowing all team members to contribute and feel valued. By fostering an environment of collaboration and creativity, Juan tapped into the team's collective potential, reigniting their enthusiasm and drive.

Establishing Progress Checkpoints

In addition to brainstorming sessions, Juan implemented regular progress checkpoints. These checkpoints served as milestones for the team to assess their progress, celebrate achievements, and identify areas for improvement. This approach was informed by research from the Harvard Business Review, which suggests that setting clear goals and providing regular feedback can enhance motivation and performance (Harvard Business Review, 2018).

By breaking down projects into smaller, manageable tasks, Juan ensured that the team could maintain focus and momentum. These checkpoints also provided opportunities for reflection and learning, allowing the team to adapt and refine their strategies as needed.

Fostering a Culture of Ownership and Accountability

To further combat Ningas Kugon, Juan fostered a culture of ownership and accountability. He encouraged team members to take responsibility for their tasks and outcomes, promoting a sense of pride and commitment. This approach was supported by studies on self-determination theory, which emphasize the importance of autonomy and intrinsic motivation in driving performance (Deci & Ryan, 2000).

By empowering his team to take charge of their work, Juan instilled a sense of purpose and dedication. This shift in mindset helped sustain motivation and engagement, as team members felt more invested in the success of their projects.

Celebrating Small Wins and Encouraging Peer Recognition

Recognizing the power of positive reinforcement, Juan made it a point to celebrate small wins and encourage peer recognition. Research by Gallup indicates that regular recognition and praise can significantly boost morale and productivity (Gallup, 2015). By acknowledging individual and team achievements, Juan reinforced the value of hard work and perseverance.

Peer recognition played a crucial role in sustaining enthusiasm. By fostering a supportive and appreciative work environment, Juan encouraged team members to acknowledge each other's contributions, strengthening bonds and building a cohesive team culture.

Leveraging Technology to Enhance Engagement

Juan also leveraged technology to enhance engagement and streamline communication. He introduced digital tools like Slack and Trello to facilitate collaboration and keep the team connected. These tools provided real-time updates and visibility into project progress, helping team members stay informed and motivated.

The integration of technology was supported by studies that demonstrate the positive impact of digital tools on productivity and team dynamics (McKinsey & Company, 2020). By providing the team with the resources they needed to succeed, Juan created an environment conducive to innovation and continuous improvement.

Balancing Autonomy and Guidance

A key aspect of Juan's approach was balancing autonomy with guidance. While he empowered his team to take ownership of their work, he also provided the necessary support and direction to ensure success. By offering mentorship and constructive feedback, Juan helped his team navigate challenges and stay on track.

This balance was informed by research on transformational leadership, which emphasizes the importance of inspiring and guiding teams while allowing them the freedom to innovate (Bass & Riggio, 2006). Juan's leadership style fostered trust and respect, creating a positive and motivating work environment.

Outcomes and Lessons Learned

Juan's strategies proved effective in overcoming Ningas Kugon and sustaining his team's enthusiasm. The regular brainstorming sessions and progress checkpoints kept the team engaged and focused, while the culture of ownership and recognition reinforced their commitment to success. As a result, the start-up experienced increased productivity, innovation, and employee satisfaction.

Juan's experience highlights the importance of understanding cultural nuances and adapting leadership strategies to address specific challenges. By fostering a supportive and empowering work environment, leaders can overcome obstacles and drive long-term success.

Conclusion: A Blueprint for Success

Juan's journey in overcoming Ningas Kugon offers valuable insights for leaders facing similar challenges in start-up environments. His approach underscores the importance of fostering creativity, maintaining motivation, and building a culture of accountability and recognition. By leveraging these strategies, leaders can unlock the full potential of their teams and achieve sustained innovation and growth.

As organizations continue to navigate the complexities of a rapidly changing world, the ability to inspire and engage teams will be critical to success. Juan's case study serves as a blueprint for leaders seeking to harness the power of cultural diversity and drive organizational excellence.

Case Study 3:
Transforming Crab Mentality into Collaborative Success

Introduction: Understanding Crab Mentality in Filipino Workplaces

Crab Mentality, a term often used in Filipino culture, describes a behavior where individuals attempt to pull down those who are succeeding, akin to crabs in a bucket. This mentality can stifle teamwork, innovation, and overall productivity within organizations. In the context of Filipino workplaces, where community and relationships hold significant value, overcoming Crab Mentality requires culturally sensitive leadership and strategic interventions.

The Role of Leadership

Effective leadership is crucial in addressing and transforming workplace dynamics. Leaders must navigate the complexities of Filipino employees' cultural values, such as utang na loob (debt of gratitude) and pakikisama (harmony), to foster a collaborative environment. This case study explores how Anna, a leader at a local marketing agency, successfully transformed Crab Mentality into a culture of collaboration and success.

Identifying the Problem: Anna's Observations

Anna noticed that Crab Mentality was deeply rooted in her agency's culture, manifesting as competitiveness, lack of support, and reluctance to share knowledge. This behavior was detrimental to the agency's teamwork and overall performance. The hierarchical nature of Filipino workplaces, coupled with a strong desire for social harmony, often led to indirect communication and unresolved conflicts, further exacerbating the issue.

The Impact on the Agency

The presence of Crab Mentality led to decreased morale, hindered creativity, and stagnant productivity. Employees were more focused on individual achievements rather than collective success, resulting in missed opportunities for innovation and growth. Anna recognized that addressing this issue was essential for the agency's long-term success.

Implementing Solutions: Culturally Relevant Strategies

Team-Building Activities

Anna introduced team-building activities designed to resonate with Filipino cultural values. These activities aimed to break down barriers, build trust, and foster a sense of community:

- **Bayanihan Workshops:** Inspired by the Filipino tradition of bayanihan, where community members come together to help one another, these workshops encouraged employees to collaborate on projects, share ideas, and support each other's growth.

- **Group Outings and Retreats:** Organizing outings and retreats helped employees bond outside the office environment, strengthening interpersonal relationships and fostering a sense of belonging.

- **Community Service Projects:** Encouraging employees to participate in community service projects instilled a sense of purpose and collective achievement, aligning with the cultural emphasis on community welfare.

Mentorship Program

Anna implemented a mentorship program that paired experienced employees with newcomers, facilitating knowledge transfer and fostering a culture of learning and growth. This program was designed with cultural sensitivity in mind:

- **Respect for Elders:** In Filipino culture, elders are highly respected, and their wisdom is valued. The mentorship program leveraged this cultural norm by positioning experienced employees as mentors, providing guidance and support to younger colleagues.

- **Communal Learning:** The program emphasized communal learning, encouraging mentors and mentees to engage in open dialogue, share experiences, and collaborate on problem-solving.

Supporting Studies and Theories

- **Social Identity Theory in the Filipino Context**

    Social Identity Theory suggests that individuals derive a sense of identity and self-esteem from their group memberships. In the Filipino workplace, fostering a collective identity can help shift focus from individual achievements to team success. By creating a strong sense of belonging and shared purpose, Anna's interventions helped mitigate the effects of Crab Mentality.

- **Psychological Safety**

    Research on psychological safety highlights the importance of creating an environment where employees feel safe to express ideas and take risks without fear of judgment. Anna's team-building activities and mentorship program contributed to a psychologically safe workplace, encouraging open communication and collaboration.

- **Collaborative Learning**

    Studies on collaborative learning demonstrate its effectiveness in enhancing team dynamics and productivity. By facilitating opportunities for employees to learn from one another, Anna's mentorship program promoted skill development and innovation, driving the agency's success.

Outcomes and Benefits

Improved Teamwork. Anna's initiatives led to significant improvements in teamwork. Employees became more supportive of each other, sharing knowledge and working collaboratively towards common goals. The agency experienced a shift from a competitive to a cooperative culture, enhancing overall team dynamics.

Increased Productivity. The transformation from Crab Mentality to collaborative success resulted in increased productivity. With a focus on collective achievement, employees were more motivated to contribute to the agency's success, leading to improved project outcomes and client satisfaction.

Enhanced Employee Satisfaction. As a result of the cultural shift, employee satisfaction and retention rates improved. Employees felt valued, supported, and part of a cohesive team, reducing turnover and fostering a positive work environment.

Challenges and Adjustments

Initial Resistance. Implementing these changes was not without challenges. Anna faced initial resistance from employees who were accustomed to the existing culture. Overcoming this required patience, persistence, and continuous communication to demonstrate the benefits of the new initiatives.

Continuous Improvement. Anna recognized the need for continuous improvement and adaptation of the programs to better meet the evolving needs of her team. Regular feedback sessions and open dialogues were conducted to refine the strategies and ensure their effectiveness.

Conclusion: Long-Term Impact and Broader Implications

Anna's efforts in transforming Crab Mentality into collaborative success had a profound long-term impact on the agency. The cultural shift not only improved teamwork and productivity but also created a supportive and inclusive work environment. This case study serves as a valuable example for other organizations seeking to navigate and overcome the complexities of Filipino workplace dynamics.

Organizations can draw valuable insights from Anna's approach, applying similar culturally sensitive strategies to foster collaboration and success. By understanding and addressing the unique cultural factors at play, leaders can create environments where employees thrive and achieve collective success.

Case Study 4:
Embracing Bahala Na with Strategic Planning

Introduction: Understanding Bahala Na in Filipino Work Culture

The phrase "Bahala Na" is deeply ingrained in Filipino culture, often interpreted as a form of fatalism or a "come what may" attitude. While it can foster resilience and adaptability, in a business context, it may lead to last-minute decision-making and lack of preparation. This case study explores how Pedro, a leader in a logistics company, transformed the Bahala Na mindset into strategic foresight and planning.

The Role of Leadership

In Filipino workplaces, leadership plays a crucial role in guiding employees through cultural complexities. Leaders must balance respect for traditional attitudes with the need for modern business practices. Pedro's approach demonstrates how culturally aware leadership can harness the positive aspects of Bahala Na while mitigating its potential downsides.

Identifying the Problem: Pedro's Observations

Pedro observed that the Bahala Na attitude was prevalent in his logistics company, leading to reactive decision-making and inefficiencies. Employees often relied on improvisation rather than planning, resulting in missed deadlines and compromised service quality. Recognizing the need for change, Pedro sought to instill a culture of strategic planning and accountability.

The Impact on the Company

The reliance on Bahala Na resulted in several operational challenges:

- **Inefficiencies:** Last-minute decision-making led to rushed processes and errors, affecting the company's logistics operations.

- **Stress and Burnout:** The lack of foresight created a high-pressure environment, contributing to employee stress and burnout.

- **Missed Opportunities:** The absence of strategic planning hindered the company's ability to seize market opportunities and innovate.

Implementing Solutions: Strategic Planning Workshops

Pedro introduced strategic planning workshops designed to align with Filipino cultural values and business objectives:

Cultural Sensitivity

Understanding the cultural roots of Bahala Na, Pedro framed strategic planning as a way to enhance, rather than replace, the positive aspects of this mindset. He emphasized that planning could coexist with adaptability and resilience, empowering employees to face uncertainty with confidence.

Workshop Structure

- **Goal Setting:** Workshops began with individual and team goal-setting sessions, aligning personal aspirations with organizational objectives.
- **Proactive Problem-Solving:** Employees participated in exercises that encouraged foresight and contingency planning, preparing them to anticipate and address potential challenges.
- **Accountability Frameworks:** Pedro introduced accountability mechanisms, such as regular check-ins and progress reviews, to ensure ongoing commitment to strategic goals.

Supporting Studies and Theories

- **Cultural Dimensions Theory.** Hofstede's Cultural Dimensions Theory provides insights into how cultural values influence workplace behavior. In the context of Filipino employees, understanding the balance between uncertainty avoidance and adaptability is key to effective leadership. Pedro's workshops leveraged this understanding to foster a culture of strategic foresight.

- **Change Management.** Research on change management highlights the importance of involving employees in the change process. By actively engaging his team in strategic planning, Pedro minimized resistance and built a sense of ownership and commitment to the new approach.

- **Goal-Setting Theory.** Goal-Setting Theory suggests that clear, challenging goals enhance performance. Pedro's focus on aligning individual and organizational goals motivated employees to pursue excellence and take initiative in their roles.

Outcomes and Benefits

Enhanced Planning and Efficiency. Pedro's initiatives led to significant improvements in planning and operational efficiency. Employees became more proactive, anticipating challenges and developing solutions in advance, reducing the reliance on last-minute decision-making.

- **Reduced Stress and Improved Morale.** By fostering a culture of preparedness, Pedro alleviated the stress associated with reactive decision-making. Employees felt more in control of their work, leading to improved morale and job satisfaction.

- **Increased Innovation and Opportunity Seizure.** With a strategic framework in place, the company was better positioned to identify and capitalize on market opportunities. The shift from a reactive to a proactive mindset enabled the company to innovate and grow.

Challenges and Adjustments

- **Initial Resistance**. Transitioning from a Bahala Na mindset to strategic planning required overcoming initial resistance. Pedro addressed this by demonstrating the tangible benefits of planning and involving employees in the process to gain their buy-in.

- **Continuous Improvement**. Pedro recognized the need for continuous improvement and adaptation of the workshops to meet evolving business needs. Regular feedback sessions and adjustments ensured the ongoing relevance and effectiveness of the strategic planning initiatives.

Conclusion: Long-Term Impact and Broader Implications

Pedro's efforts to transform the Bahala Na attitude into strategic foresight had a lasting impact on the company. The cultural shift not only improved operational efficiency and employee well-being but also positioned the company for sustainable growth and success. This case study serves as a valuable example for other organizations navigating the complexities of Filipino workplace dynamics.

Organizations can draw valuable insights from Pedro's approach, applying similar culturally sensitive strategies to foster strategic foresight and planning. By understanding and addressing the unique cultural factors at play, leaders can create environments where employees thrive and achieve collective success.

Tools and Resources: Equipping Managers for Success

To effectively manage Filipino teams, having the right tools and resources at your disposal is essential. Here are some practical tools and resources that can aid in ongoing learning and development:

- **Cultural Sensitivity Training**: Engage in workshops and seminars that focus on understanding Filipino culture and workplace dynamics. These programs can provide valuable insights into cultural nuances and effective communication strategies.
- **Time Management Apps**: Utilize digital tools that help track and manage time efficiently. Apps like Trello, Asana, or Slack can aid in organizing tasks and maintaining project timelines.
- **Recognition Platforms**: Implement platforms that facilitate peer recognition and reward systems. Tools like Bonusly or Kudos can help create a culture of appreciation and motivation.
- **Professional Development Programs**: Encourage continuous learning through online courses, webinars, and certifications. Platforms like Coursera, LinkedIn Learning, or Udemy offer a wide range of topics relevant to leadership and management.

Final Thoughts: Embracing Diversity as a Strength

As we draw this guide to a close, it is essential to pause and reflect on the key insights and strategies that have been shared throughout these chapters. Managing Filipino employees, with their rich cultural heritage and unique work ethic, presents a distinctive set of challenges. Yet, within these challenges lie incredible opportunities for growth, innovation, and transformation.

The Power of Cultural Diversity

Cultural diversity is not just a characteristic of the modern workplace—it is a powerful asset that, when harnessed effectively, can drive an organization to new heights. Filipino employees bring a wealth of experiences, perspectives, and talents that enrich the fabric of any team. By embracing these differences, you cultivate an environment where creativity thrives, collaboration flourishes, and innovation becomes the norm.

Creating an Inclusive Workplace

An inclusive workplace is one where every individual feels valued, respected, and empowered to contribute their best. As a leader, your role is to create such an environment, where the unique qualities of each team member are recognized and celebrated. This involves not only understanding cultural nuances but also fostering open communication, mutual respect, and a shared vision for success.

Inspiring and Empowering Your Team

Effective leadership goes beyond the mere achievement of goals. It is about inspiring and empowering your team to reach their full potential. This means providing the support, resources, and opportunities needed for personal and professional growth. By doing so, you build a team that is not only capable but also motivated and committed to achieving great things together.

The Ever-Evolving Journey of Leadership

The journey of leadership is a continuous process of learning, adaptation, and growth. As you navigate the complexities of managing a diverse team, remain open to new ideas, perspectives, and approaches. Embrace the lessons learned from both successes and challenges, and use them to refine your leadership style and strategies.

A Call to Action

Whether you are leading a team in the bustling heart of Manila or managing Overseas Filipino Workers (OFWs) across the globe, embrace the complexities and celebrate the successes that come with managing a culturally diverse workforce. Recognize the invaluable contributions of your Filipino employees, and work towards creating a workplace that is inclusive, innovative, and dynamic.

Conclusion: Leading with Confidence and Grace

As you move forward in your leadership journey, carry with you the insights and strategies shared in this guide. With the right mindset and tools, you can navigate the complexities of managing a diverse team with confidence and grace. Remember, the true measure of leadership is not just in the goals achieved, but in the positive impact you have on the lives of those you lead.

Epilogue:
Navigating the Future

As we close this guide, it's clear that leading Filipino employees is both an art and a science, enriched by cultural understanding and strategic insight. The journey through this book has highlighted the complexities and strengths of the Filipino workforce, offering a roadmap to effective leadership.

The vibrant tapestry of the Philippines, with its diverse islands and rich cultural heritage, mirrors the dynamic nature of its people. By embracing these complexities, you unlock the potential for innovation, collaboration, and success within your team.

As you apply the insights and strategies shared in this book, remember that leadership is an evolving journey. Continue to learn, adapt, and celebrate the unique qualities of your team. By doing so, you not only enhance your leadership skills but also contribute to a more inclusive and harmonious workplace.

Thank you for embarking on this journey with us. May your leadership path be filled with growth, understanding, and fulfillment.

The Role of Religion in Motivating Filipino Employees

Christianity is the majority religion in the Philippines, with over 90% of the population identifying as Christian, and the majority being Roman Catholic. This deep-rooted faith significantly influences the behavior and motivations of Filipino employees.

For many Filipinos, religion is a central aspect of life that shapes values, ethics, and daily interactions. The Christian faith, particularly Catholicism, emphasizes community, compassion, and service, which are reflected in the workplace. Employees often draw motivation from their religious beliefs, finding purpose and meaning in their work as a form of service to others and a way to honor their faith.

How Religion Influences Workplace Behavior

Community and Cooperation: The emphasis on community in Christian teachings encourages cooperation and teamwork among Filipino employees. This can lead to a supportive and collaborative work environment where individuals are motivated to help one another and work towards common goals.

Integrity and Ethics: Christian values promote honesty, integrity, and ethical behavior. Filipino employees may be motivated to uphold these principles in their professional conduct, striving to maintain trust and respect within the workplace.

Resilience and Optimism: Faith often provides a source of strength and optimism, helping employees navigate challenges with resilience. This positive outlook can enhance motivation and perseverance, contributing to a more dynamic and productive work environment.

Considerations for Managers

As a manager of Filipino employees, it's important to recognize and respect the role of religion in their lives. While this topic isn't covered in detail in this book, it will be explored thoroughly in my next book, *"Inspired by Faith: How Christianity Shapes Filipino Employee Motivation."*

Please stay tuned on the release of the said book.

ANNEX SECTION

The History of the Philippines: How it Shaped the Behavior of Filipino Employees.

A brief background on the history of the Philippines will help you understand how it influenced the behavior, trait, and attitude of Filipino employees.

Pre-Colonial Period

Before the arrival of colonizers, the Philippines was a collection of independent barangays (small communities) led by local chieftains called datus. These communities engaged in trade with neighboring regions, such as China and the Malay Archipelago. The social structure was hierarchical, but there was a strong sense of community and cooperation, traits that continue to influence Filipino work culture today.

Influence on Work Behavior:

Community and Cooperation: The pre-colonial emphasis on community cooperation is reflected in the Filipino value of "bayanihan," or communal unity, which is evident in teamwork and collaboration in the workplace.

Spanish Colonization (1521-1898)

The Spanish colonization began with Ferdinand Magellan's arrival in 1521 and lasted for over 300 years. The Spaniards introduced Christianity, which became deeply ingrained in Filipino culture. They also implemented a centralized government and feudal system, which significantly altered the social structure.

Influence of Spanish Regime on Filipino Work Behavior:

Religion and Ethics: The introduction of Christianity instilled values of compassion, service, and integrity, which are reflected in the ethical behavior of Filipino employees.

Hierarchy and Respect: The Spanish colonial system emphasized hierarchy and authority, influencing the respect for leadership and seniority in Filipino workplaces.

American Colonization (1898-1946)

Following the Spanish-American War, the Philippines became a U.S. territory. The Americans introduced public education, infrastructure development, and democratic governance. English became the medium of instruction, and American cultural influences permeated Filipino society.

Influence of American Regime on Work Behavior:

Education and Professionalism: The American emphasis on education laid the foundation for a skilled and educated workforce, contributing to the professionalism of Filipino employees.

Adaptability and Resilience: Exposure to diverse cultural influences fostered adaptability and resilience, traits that are highly valued in the global workforce.

Japanese Occupation (1942-1945)

During World War II, the Philippines was occupied by Japan. This period was marked by hardship and resistance, as Filipinos fought for their freedom and independence.

Influence of Japanese Regime on Filipino Work Behavior:

Resilience and Determination: The struggle for survival during the occupation instilled resilience and determination, qualities that are evident in the perseverance of Filipino employees.

Post-Independence Era (1946-Present)

After gaining independence in 1946, the Philippines faced political and economic challenges. The country experienced periods of growth and instability, including the martial law era under Ferdinand Marcos and the People Power Revolution of 1986.

How this Era is Shaping Employees' Work Behavior:

Innovation and Initiative: The post-independence era fostered a spirit of innovation and initiative, as Filipinos sought to rebuild and improve their nation.

Social Responsibility: The People Power Revolution highlighted the importance of social responsibility and civic engagement, values that influence the ethical behavior of Filipino employees.

The Growth of Overseas Filipino Workers (OFWs)

Origins and Early Development

The migration of Filipinos for work began in the early 20th century, with laborers traveling to Hawaii and the United States for agricultural jobs. However, the modern OFW phenomenon took shape in the 1970s, driven by economic challenges and the demand for labor abroad.

Key Developments:

1970s Oil Boom: The oil boom in the Middle East created a demand for labor, leading to the deployment of Filipino workers in construction and domestic services.

Government Initiatives: The Philippine government established agencies to facilitate overseas employment, recognizing it as a solution to domestic unemployment and a source of foreign remittances.

Evolving Roles and Professional Growth

Initially, many Filipinos took on roles as domestic helpers and laborers. However, over time, the landscape of OFW employment evolved, with an increasing number of Filipinos taking on professional roles in various fields.

Current Trends:

Diverse Professions: Today, Filipinos work in diverse professions, including healthcare, engineering, information technology, and education. This shift reflects the growing recognition of Filipino skills and expertise on the global stage.

Professional Development: The emphasis on education and training has enabled Filipinos to pursue higher-level positions and specialized roles, enhancing their career prospects and earning potential.

Impact on the Philippine Economy and Society

OFWs have become a vital part of the Philippine economy, contributing significantly through remittances. These funds support families, drive economic growth, and contribute to national development.

Social and Economic Impact:

Economic Contribution: Remittances from OFWs account for a substantial portion of the country's GDP, providing financial stability for families and communities.

Cultural Exchange: The global presence of Filipinos fosters cultural exchange and enhances the Philippines' reputation as a source of skilled and adaptable workers.

Conclusion: The Legacy of History and the Future of Filipino Employees

The history of the Philippines has profoundly shaped the behavior and culture of Filipino employees. From the communal values of pre-colonial times to the resilience learned during periods of colonization and occupation, these historical influences continue to impact the Filipino workforce.

The growth of OFWs reflects the adaptability and determination of Filipinos to seek opportunities and contribute globally. As the landscape of overseas employment evolves, Filipinos continue to excel in diverse fields, showcasing their professionalism and dedication.

As we look to the future, the lessons of history remind us of the importance of cultural understanding and appreciation. By embracing the unique qualities of Filipino employees, organizations can foster inclusive and dynamic workplaces that harness the strengths of this vibrant workforce.

The Map of the Philippines

Image source: https://www.freepik.com/

The Regions of the Philippines: Diversity and Its Impact on Filipino Employees

The Philippines, an archipelago of over 7,000 islands, is divided into 18 regions, each with its own distinct cultural identity, language, and traditions. This diversity is a testament to the country's rich history and varied influences, shaping the behavior and traits of Filipino employees across different regions.

Understanding Regional Diversity

Each region in the Philippines has developed its own unique culture, influenced by geography, historical events, and interactions with other cultures. From the bustling urban centers of Metro Manila to the serene landscapes of the Cordilleras, these regional differences contribute to a vibrant national tapestry.

- **Luzon:** Known for its economic and political significance, Luzon is home to the capital, Manila, and is a melting pot of cultures and languages. The influence of Spanish and American colonization is evident in its architecture and traditions.

- **Visayas:** Famous for its festivals and beaches, the Visayas region is known for its warm hospitality and vibrant cultural expressions. The people here are often multilingual, speaking a mix of Cebuano, Hiligaynon, and Waray.

- **Mindanao:** With its diverse ethnic groups and natural resources, Mindanao is a land of contrasts. The region's rich cultural heritage is reflected in its music, dance, and traditional crafts.

Impact on Filipino Employees

The regional diversity of the Philippines influences the behavior and traits of Filipino employees in several ways:

- **Adaptability and Resilience:** Growing up in diverse environments, Filipinos are naturally adaptable and resilient. These traits are valuable in the workplace, allowing them to navigate challenges and changes with ease.

- **Community and Cooperation:** The sense of community is strong across all regions, fostering teamwork and collaboration among employees. This communal spirit is reflected in the workplace, where cooperation and mutual support are highly valued.

- **Cultural Sensitivity:** Exposure to various cultural practices and languages enhances Filipinos' cultural sensitivity. This ability to understand and respect differences is crucial in multicultural work environments.

- **Regionalism:** Filipinos often exhibit regionalism, a sense of pride and loyalty to their home region. This can influence workplace dynamics, as employees may bring regional perspectives and preferences to their roles.

Conclusion: Embracing Diversity in the Workplace

The regional diversity of the Philippines is a source of strength and resilience for Filipino employees. By understanding and embracing these differences, managers can create inclusive workplaces that celebrate the unique qualities of their team members. Recognizing the impact of regionalism and cultural diversity can lead to more effective leadership and a harmonious work environment.

As the Philippines continues to evolve, its rich regional tapestry will remain a vital part of its national identity, shaping the behavior and traits of its people, both at home and abroad.

The Overseas Filipino Workers (OFWs)

The regional diversity of the Philippines also plays a role in the growth of Overseas Filipino Workers (OFWs). Historically, economic opportunities have varied across regions, prompting many Filipinos to seek work abroad. Initially, many OFWs took on roles as domestic helpers, but today, they are recognized for their skills in various professional fields.

- **Professional Growth:** The emphasis on education and training has enabled Filipinos from all regions to pursue careers in healthcare, engineering, and technology, among others.

- **Cultural Ambassadors:** OFWs serve as cultural ambassadors, sharing their regional customs and traditions with the world, enhancing the global perception of the Philippines.

As of recent data, approximately 2.16 million OFWs are spread across the world, contributing to various industries and economies.

Top Destinations for OFWs

The Middle East remains a focal point for Filipino workers, with Saudi Arabia hosting about 23% of the total OFW population. The demand for labor in construction and domestic services has made Saudi Arabia a top destination. Other key countries include the United Arab Emirates, Singapore, Hong Kong, and Qatar, each offering diverse opportunities for Filipino workers.

Diverse Occupations and Contributions

OFWs are employed in a wide range of occupations, reflecting their adaptability and skills:

- **Elementary Occupations**: Comprising 41.1% of OFWs, this category includes domestic helpers and laborers. These roles are crucial in supporting households and industries across host countries.

- **Service and Sales Workers**: These workers are integral to the hospitality and retail sectors, providing essential services and enhancing customer experiences.

- **Professionals:** A significant number of OFWs are professionals in healthcare, engineering, and education. Their expertise is increasingly recognized globally, highlighting the Philippines as a source of skilled talent.

- **Technicians and Associate Professionals**: These roles involve specialized skills and technical knowledge, contributing to various industries such as IT and telecommunications.

Key Insights and Trends

- Saudi Arabia as a Leading Destination: The demand for construction workers and domestic helpers keeps Saudi Arabia at the forefront of OFW destinations. The country's economic projects and household needs continue to attract Filipino workers.

- Recognition of Professional Skills: While elementary occupations constitute a large portion of OFW roles, there is a growing presence of Filipino professionals. The healthcare and engineering sectors have seen an influx of skilled Filipino workers, underscoring the global recognition of their capabilities.

- Economic Contributions: OFWs play a vital role in the Philippine economy through remittances, which support families and drive national development. Their earnings contribute significantly to the country's GDP, providing financial stability for many households.

Challenges and Opportunities

Despite their contributions, OFWs face challenges such as cultural adaptation, separation from families, and sometimes unfavorable working conditions. However, the Philippine government and various organizations continue to provide support through policies and programs aimed at protecting their rights and welfare.

The global demand for skilled workers presents opportunities for more Filipinos to pursue careers abroad, enhancing their professional growth and contributing to international communities.

As the world becomes increasingly interconnected, the role of OFWs in bridging cultures and economies will only grow more significant.

Conclusion

The story of Overseas Filipino Workers is one of resilience, adaptability, and global impact. As they continue to make their mark in diverse fields and countries, OFWs embody the spirit of the Philippines—dedicated, skilled, and ever-ready to contribute to the world. Their journey not only supports their families but also enriches the global workforce, making them invaluable ambassadors of Filipino talent and culture.

The Global Footprint of Filipino Migrants

Overseas Filipino Workers (OFWs) specifically refer to Filipinos who are working abroad on temporary contracts. They are distinct from Filipino migrants or immigrants who have permanently moved to another country and may have obtained residency or citizenship there. OFWs typically return to the Philippines after their employment contracts end.

As of recent estimates, there are approximately 10 to 12 million Filipino migrants worldwide. This includes those who have permanently settled abroad, obtained residency, or citizenship in countries such as the United States, Canada, Australia, and various European nations.

Filipinos are scattered across the globe, weaving their rich cultural tapestry into the fabric of countless communities. As they build families and transfer their cherished traditions to new lands, they contribute significantly to the development of these countries. From arts and science to politics and cuisine, Filipino migrants are making their mark on the world stage.

A Global Presence

The Filipino diaspora is vast and diverse, with millions of migrants calling various continents home. This widespread presence reflects the adaptability and resilience of Filipinos as they seek opportunities and build new lives abroad.

- **Asia**: Approximately 3 to 4 million Filipinos reside in countries like Japan, South Korea, and Singapore. They play vital roles in industries such as healthcare, technology, and education, while also sharing Filipino culture through festivals and community events.

- **North America**: With an estimated 4 to 5 million Filipinos, North America hosts the largest concentration of Filipino migrants. In the United States and Canada, Filipinos excel in various fields, including healthcare, engineering, and the arts. Their influence extends to politics, with Filipino-Americans holding public office and advocating for community interests.

- **Europe:** Around 1 to 2 million Filipinos have settled in Europe, with significant populations in the United Kingdom, Italy, and Spain. They contribute to sectors such as healthcare, hospitality, and education, while also enriching the cultural landscape with Filipino music, dance, and cuisine.

- **Australia and Oceania:** Approximately 300,000 to 400,000 Filipinos live in Australia and New Zealand. They are active in professions like nursing, education, and information technology, bringing their skills and vibrant culture to these regions.

- **Middle East:** About 1 million Filipinos reside in the Middle East, particularly in countries like Saudi Arabia and the United Arab Emirates. They are integral to industries such as construction, hospitality, and healthcare, while also maintaining strong cultural ties through community organizations and events.

Cultural Ambassadors

Filipino migrants serve as cultural ambassadors, introducing their rich heritage to diverse audiences. They share traditional Filipino dishes, such as adobo and lumpia, through restaurants and food festivals, offering a taste of the Philippines to the world. Cultural events and performances showcase Filipino music, dance, and art, fostering cross-cultural understanding and appreciation.

Contributions to Arts, Science, and Politics

Filipinos are making significant contributions to the fields of arts, science, and politics. In the arts, Filipino musicians, filmmakers, and visual artists are gaining international recognition, bringing Filipino stories and perspectives to global audiences. In science, Filipino researchers and professionals are advancing knowledge and innovation in areas such as medicine, technology, and environmental studies.

Politically, Filipino migrants are becoming more engaged, with some assuming leadership roles in their adopted countries. Their participation in political processes helps shape policies and advocate for the rights and interests of the Filipino community.

Building Bridges and Communities

The presence of Filipino migrants worldwide is not just about economic contributions; it's about building bridges and fostering communities. Through their resilience, work ethic, and warmth, Filipinos are creating inclusive and supportive environments that celebrate diversity and promote mutual respect.

Conclusion

The global footprint of Filipino migrants is a testament to their adaptability, resilience, and cultural richness. As they continue to build families, share traditions, and contribute to various fields, Filipinos are enhancing the global community with their unique blend of talent, culture, and spirit. Their journey is one of growth, connection, and empowerment, leaving a lasting impact on the world.

About the Author

Angelo Villamejor is a seasoned leader and cultural enthusiast, renowned for fostering inclusive and dynamic workplaces. With a rich and diverse career spanning the insurance, banking, and travel industries, Angelo brings a wealth of experience in managing and leading diverse teams. This extensive background has equipped Angelo with a deep understanding of the unique cultural nuances that influence employee interactions and performance.

As the CEO of Onenetworx, Angelo has successfully navigated the complexities of leading Filipino employees, drawing on a wealth of knowledge and practical insights. Onenetworx, founded in 2011, has evolved from a small office-garage operation into a pioneering company specializing in marketing and sales outsourcing. Under Angelo's leadership, the company has embraced a mission to provide livelihood opportunities to marginalized sectors in the Philippines through innovative home-based employment programs and strategic partnerships.

Angelo's commitment to cultural sensitivity and strategic leadership has made them a respected figure in the field of human resources and organizational development. Their leadership style emphasizes the importance of aligning organizational goals with cultural values, fostering an environment where employees thrive and achieve collective success.

Angelo has been instrumental in transforming Onenetworx into a multi-product marketing company, expanding its offerings to include non-life insurance, life insurance, and HMO products. The company's unique recruitment, training, and management programs for sales personnel have set a benchmark in the industry, ensuring a productive and motivated salesforce.

With a focus on continuous growth and innovation, Angelo Villamejor remains committed to leading Onenetworx towards new horizons, exploring opportunities in international markets and expanding product lines. Their journey exemplifies the power of strategic leadership and cultural understanding in driving organizational success.

Through "A Guide to Leading (and Surviving) the Complexities of Filipino Employees," Angelo shares their expertise and vision, offering valuable guidance to managers and leaders worldwide. When not writing or leading teams, Angelo enjoys exploring the vibrant landscapes of the Philippines and connecting with its rich cultural heritage.

www.ingramcontent.com/pod-product-compliance
Lightning Source LLC
Chambersburg PA
CBHW082251220526
45469CB00009B/2966